Raisins and Almonds

Edited by Henry and Marie Einspruch

THE LEWIS AND HARRIET LEDERER FOUNDATION
6204 Park Heights Avenue Baltimore, Maryland 21215

ACKNOWLEDGMENTS

Third Edition

Library of Congress Catalog Card Number: 67-19843

Printed in the U.S.A.

Illustrations:

Cover Page from Abraham Goldfaden's Opera *Shulamith*.
Devastation, p. 41, used by permission of Wide World Photos, Inc.
Drawings by E. M. Lilien
The Fiddler, p. 47, by Isidor Kaufmann

Some of the material in this collection has appeared in previous publications. We give credit to *The Mediator* and *Hymns of Faith*. All unsigned articles are from the pen of the editors.

CONTENTS

Introduction

The title "Raisins and Almonds" was suggested by the well-known Jewish folk song (popularized by Abraham Goldfaden in his opera *Shulamith*), which many of us associate with the dreams, joys, and promise of good things to come.

In selecting the contents for this book we tried to pick material on a variety of subjects. Included are essays, poetry, biographies, hymns, as well as discussions on some of the weightier issues of life.

"Raisins and Almonds" is a little bit of this and that, and we hope our readers will find something to bite into.

The Editors

What Must the World Think of Us?

"Half the world worships a Jew, the other half a Jewess," rang through the halls of the British Parliament when Disraeli was taunted with his Jewish birth. It was a just comeback, a telling reminder of the world's spiritual debt to Israel.

Where are the great of yesterday? Olympus is emptied of its inhabitants; Isis and Osiris, Baal and Jupiter, are but memories of a forgotten past; Socrates, Plato, Aristotle, and the heroes of antiquity faded into the background upon the entrance of a Judean on the arena of history.

Is it not strange that the Jew, Jesus of Nazareth, should not only have captured the imagination and heart of the world, but even superseded its national heroes? For, towering above Washington and Lincoln, looms Jesus, the Jew, in the estimation of the people of America. Greater than Shakespeare or Darwin is the significance of Jesus to the people of England. And, in the words of Dr. Ḥaim Zhitlowsky, the Jewish savant, "Far greater than Spinoza, greater than Karl Marx, greater even than the prophets is this Jesus of ours." Dos NAYE LEBEN, Vol. I, p. 741.

Does it mean nothing to us that mankind reveres "flesh of our flesh and bone of our bone"? If Jesus were an American and all the world except America would pay homage to him, we would say that America was stupid.

What must the world think of us?

The Message of Ruth

By MOSES SCHAPIRO

The book of Ruth contains one of the most fascinating stories in the Bible, and there are few more outstanding characters in the entire portrait gallery of Scripture, than those portrayed in this captivating narrative, simple, pastoral and human.

Sweetness and light seem to radiate from the story, and there is appeal to the highest attributes of human sympathy and unselfishness, that touch of nature which makes the whole world kin.

The book of Ruth is by no means a purely Jewish one, and it teaches lessons that are more needed now than ever. The tragedy of the world today is lack of love, and it is urgent to emphasize the fact that "no man is an island," for the destiny of the individual is bound up with that of the race.

As a matter of fact, the book of Ruth contains no legislation, no statutes of prohibition or dealing with forbidden things. It has nothing to do with prophecy, ordinances, state polity or any other subject than love. As the *Midrash* says:

"This roll contains neither things clean or unclean, things permitted or prohibited. But why was it written? To tell us how much reward is reserved for those who show mercy."

„מגלה זו אין בה לא טומאה ולא טהרה, ולא איסור ולא היתר; ולמה נכתבה? ללמדך, כמה שכר טוב לגומלי חסדים" (מדרש רבה, רות, פרשה ב, טו).

The entire narrative is one of winning simplicity, depicting affection, industry, humility, happiness. The book is written in language pure and beautiful, and its human sincerity charms the reader of simple tastes, as well as the man of culture. Manners and customs have altered—some will say advanced—beyond the setting of this Biblical story, but the picture is as vivid today as then; for in matters of the heart and emotions, the same age-long threads run through the whole fabric of humanity.

The compelling interest in Ruth, the Moabite heroine, centers in the fact that she, a pagan woman, became a connecting link between Jew and Gentile as the ancestress of King David, and thus of Jesus, the Saviour of the world.

Isaac Lichtenstein

District Rabbi of Tapio-Szele, Hungary

"I had thought the New Testament to be impure, a source of pride, of hatred, and of the worst kind of violence, but as I opened it, I felt myself peculiarly and wonderfully taken possession of.

"A sudden glory, a light, flashed through my soul. I looked for thorns, and gathered roses; I discovered pearls instead of pebbles; instead of hatred, love; instead of vengeance, forgiveness; instead of bondage, freedom; instead of pride, humility; instead of enmity, conciliation; instead of death, life, salvation, resurrection, heavenly treasure."

A Walker in the City

By ALFRED KAZIN

Look how much light there is. It does not matter now that the sun is so fierce, it burns your feet on the iron planks; that when you get up to stretch your legs, the heat makes you so dizzy, you can see yourself falling down the red-painted ladders that chase each other to the street. For now a single line of English words takes you up slowly, and slowly carries you across the page to where, each time you reach its end, you have to catch your breath and look away—the pleasure is unbearable, it is so full.

But when that which is perfect is come, then that which is in part shall be done away.

When I was a child, I spake as a child, I understood as a child, I thought as a child; but when I became a man, I put away childish things.

For now we see through a glass, darkly: but then face to face: now I know in part; but then shall I know even as also I am known.

The man from whom I had accepted the little blue volume on the Fifth Avenue steps of the library had said to me in Yiddish, searching my face doubtfully: "You *are* a Jew? You will really look into it?" No, I was not really looking into it; I could not read more than two or three pages at a time without turning away in excitement and shame. Would the old women across the street ever have believed it?

How square and hardy the words looked in their even black type. Each seemed to burn separately in the sun as I nervously flipped the pages and then turned back to where the book most naturally lay flat:

For now we see through a glass, darkly.

Each time my eye fell on that square even black type, the sentence began to move in the sun. It rose up, a smoking frame of dark glass above the highest roofs, steadily and joyfully burning, as, reading aloud to myself, I tasted the rightness of each word on my tongue.

It was like heaping my own arms with gifts. There were images I did not understand, but which fell on my mind with such slow opening grandeur that once I distinctly heard the clean and fundamental cracking of trees. . . . Images were instantaneous; the meaning alone could be like the unyielding metal taste when you bit on an empty spoon. . . . But now, each day I turned back to that little blue Testament, I had that same sense of instant connectedness I had already noticed in myself to the exclamation O *altitudo!* in a quotation from Sir Thomas Browne; to the chapter on the cathedral in Lawrence's *The Rainbow;* to the opening line of Henry Vaughan's "The World,"

I saw Eternity the other night

that haunted me from the day I came on it in an anthology; to Blake's

When the stars threw down their spears
And water'd heaven with their tears,
Did he smile his work to see?
Did he who made the Lamb make thee?

to the opening lines of A *Farewell to Arms*, indescribably dry and beautiful with the light on those pebbles in the plain; to *When Lilacs Last in the Dooryard Bloom'd*, where I knew as soon as I came on the line

Passing the yellow-spear'd wheat, every grain from its shroud in the dark brown fields uprisen—

that I had found another writer I could instinctively trust.

First the image, then the sense. First those clouds moving blue and white across the nearest roofs; and then—O *altitudo!*, the journey into that other land of *flax*, of summer, eternal summer, through which *he* had walked, wrapped in a blue and white prayer shawl, and, still looking back at me with the heartbreaking smile of recognition from a fellow Jew, had said:

The blind receive their sight, and the lame walk, the lepers are cleansed, and the deaf hear, the dead are raised up, and the poor have the gospel preached to them.

And blessed is he, whosoever shall not be offended in me.

Offended in him? I had known him instantly. Surely I had been waiting for him all my life—our own Yeshua, misunderstood by his own, like me, but the very embodiment of everything I had waited so long to hear from a Jew—a great contempt for the minute daily business of the world; a deep and joyful turning back into our own spirit. It was *he*, I thought, who would resolve for me at last the ambiguity and the long ache of being a Jew—Yeshua, our own long-lost Jesus, speaking straight to the mind and heart at once . . . .

How long I had been waiting for him, how long: like metal for a magnet to raise it. I had recognized him immediately, and all over: that exaltation; those thorny images that cut you with their overriding fervor and gave you the husk of every word along with the kernel; that furious old Jewish impatience with *Success*, with comfort, with eating, with the rich, with the whole shabby superficial fashionable world itself; that fatigue, as of a man having constantly to make his way up and down the world on foot; and then that sternness and love that gushed out of him when he turned to the others and said:

For verily I say unto you, Till heaven and earth pass, one jot or one tittle shall in no wise pass from the Law, till all be fulfilled.

Yeshua my Yeshua! What had he to do with those who killed his own and worshipped him as God? Why would *they* call him only by that smooth Greek name of Jesus? He was Yeshua, my own Reb Yeshua, of whose terrible death I could never read without bursting into tears—Yeshua, our own Yeshua, the most natural of us all, the most direct, the most enchanted, and as he sprang up from the heart of poor Jews, all the dearer to me because he could now return to his own kind: *and the poor have the gospel preached to them.*

De Profundis

"Out of the depths have I cried unto Thee, O Lord!"
Psalm 130

We've torn the perils from the sky,
The secrets from the sod,
We've chained the lightning to our wheel,
And called the man-thing God.
On heights we stand, while at our feet
We watch the storm clouds roll,
But, oh, Thou thorn-crowned Nazarene,
Have mercy on our soul.

I have no God to call my own,
No Saviour hears my prayer,
No kind Redeemer claims my soul
Its blackened sins to bear.
There are no hands to lift me up,
No wings on which to soar,
There's only me, there's only me,
Just me, and nothing more.

My zero hour of despair
Is mine, and mine alone;
All mine the darkness of the pit,
The glory of the throne.
All mine, my life, to make or mar,
To conquer or to fail,
And none but me own equity
Where I, myself, break trail.

Through trackless seas I plough my way,
By nameless stars I steer,
A broken rudder keeps my course,
My mates are doubt and fear.
No Pilot guides my chartless drift,
No compass holds me true,
Oh, Captain of the portless ship,
Have mercy on the crew!

There is no Fountain filled with blood
To wash my sins away,
There is no Comforter by night,
No shadowed Rock by day;
I wander through the desert land
Where shapes affrighted stroll,
And Thou, O Thou, who know'st me not,
Have mercy on my soul.

There is no Face in pity bent
When by the way I fall,
No anxious, loving Shepherd comes
In answer to my call.
There are no tender eyes to seek,
No gentle arms to hold,
No nail-pierced hands to take me up
And bring me to the fold.

And when on naked, bleeding feet
To Calvary I go,
And stagger, crushed, beneath the cross,
There's none to heed or know;
There's none to lift the cruel weight,
There's none to even share,
Oh, Thou, who climbed the Hill before
Look down and help me bear.

Oh, Thou who feared, yet drained the cup
Of valed Gethsemane,
Who hung from torn and bleeding palms
And died, like that, for me,
Oh, Thou, if Thou can'st understand,
Forgive, forgive, atone,
Unto my outcast soul that drifts
Alone, alone, alone.

By scales that weigh the universe,
By rule that measures time,
By law that knows no compromise
With blood, not love, nor rhyme,
By lead that plumbs the spaceless void,
By reason's shackles rive,
Oh, Thou, O Thou, whom we deny,
Have mercy and forgive.

Si Tannhauser

I Went to Synagogue

By JACOB FRIEDMAN

I hadn't been to synagogue for many years. I often pass them, but when they are open I haven't time to go in, and when I have time they are closed.

On New Year's and Yom Kippur one can't go to synagogue without a ticket. This year I bought a ticket, and did not regret it. In the first place, there was some excellent singing, and what I experienced was worth more than it cost me.

Did I join in the prayers? Of course I did. True, I was ill at ease when I came to: "Blessed art Thou, O Lord our God, King of the Universe, who hast not made me a woman." Such peacock-like gloating on the part of the male of the species was, I thought, a little out of place when addressing the Deity.

I smote my breast as I asked Divine pardon: "For the sin wherein we have sinned before Thee by the profanation of Thy Name . . . . For the sin wherein we have sinned before Thee by envy" . . . . There wasn't anything in the long catalogue of sins in the Prayer Book to which I could not plead guilty, although I knew full well that a year hence, if I live, I would be doing precisely the same things all over again—envying, ripping up my neighbor, and so forth.

Strange that I should get to thinking about Jesus in the synagogue. I sometimes think about him, and particularly of that saying of his: "If you do not forgive men their sins, neither will your Father in heaven forgive your sins." He was a dreamer, for he not only insisted that we love our neighbor, but also our enemy. It's hard enough to love your neighbor—let alone your enemy! And yet we expect God to forgive us when we are not ready to do it ourselves.

I looked in the direction of Joe Levy; he's my competitor, and we haven't spoken to one another for a long time. "Try the Jesus idea on him, he's your enemy, and you must love him."

When I walked over and extended my hand, he almost collapsed. To my wishing him a Happy New Year, he rejoined, in a voice trembling with emotion, "The same to you, and may you be inscribed in the Book of Life."

I was glad I went to synagogue.

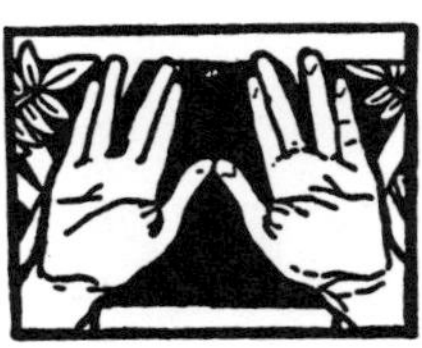

The Song of Simeon Ha-Tzadik

Lord, now lettest thou thy servant depart in peace,
According to thy word;
For my eyes have seen thy salvation
Which thou hast prepared before the face of all peoples,
A light to lighten the Gentiles,
And the glory of thy people Israel.

The Gospel According to Luke 2:29-32

דאָס געזאַנג פֿון שׁמעון הַצַדיק

אַצינד טוסטו אָפּלאָזן דײַן קנעכט, אָ גאָט,
לויט דײַן וואָרט, בשָׁלום;
וואָרים מײַנע אויגן האָבן געזען דײַן ישועה,
וואָס דו האָסט אָנגעברייט פֿאַר אַלע פֿעלקער;
אַ ליכט צו באַלײַכטן די אומות,
און דער כָּבוד פֿון דיין פֿאָלק ישׂרָאל.

די בשׂורה לויט לוקאַס ב׳: 29—32

A Most Important Book

Writing in DER WEG (The Way), a Yiddish daily of Mexico City, Melech Ravitch, distinguished poet and literary critic, presents the following review of "A Most Important Book."

It was most likely a coincidence that a truly beautiful translation of the New Testament into Yiddish made its apperance soon after the publication of Yehoash's Yiddish version of the Old Testament. Yehoash's work is not easy to evaluate. The Bible has been translated into more than a thousand languages and dialects—and even in Yiddish we have had several versions of it. But it was not until Yehoash put his hand to the task that a scholarly rendition of the Old Testament became available in the *lingua Franca* of millions of Jews.

The present translation of the New Testament into Yiddish was made by Dr. Henry Einspruch. His work is unquestionably beautiful. One feels that the translator is familiar with modern Yiddish literature, and that he is master of the finest nuances of the language. In comparison with previous translations, this is truly an outstanding work.

For well known reasons the New Testament has remained for many of us Jews a book sealed with seven seals. And that is truly a pity, for to some seven hundred million people it is a sacred book. A cultured person should know such a work; I myself have read it and recommend it to every intelligent Jew.

The New Testament is divided into twenty-seven books. Some of them contain eighty pages, while others, like Paul's letter to Philemon, consists of only two. The same is true of the Old Testament. Among its thirty-nine books are some which take up a hundred or more pages, whereas the Prophet Obadiah takes up only two.

Among the twenty-seven books of the New Testament are four Gospels: Matthew, Mark, Luke and John. These are followed by the Acts of the Apostles. Then come twenty-one letters or epistles, thirteen of which are from the pen of Paul. There is also a letter to the Hebrews. Seven letters are by other writers. At the end comes the Book of Revelation.

The most important part of the book are the four Gospels, in which is told the story of Jesus, his birth, teachings, death, and resurrection. The question might be asked, why tell the same story four different times? To this there are four times four thousand answers. This method of telling the same story in several versions and then bringing them together in one book is quite familiar to us Jews. It was no less familiar to the writers of the Gospels. It is generally assumed that Matthew wrote his Gospel for Jews, Mark for the Romans, Luke for the Greeks, and John for humanity at large.

To compare the New Testament with the Old Testament is impossible. At most the New Testament is a branch of the Old Testament, and was written by men who nowhere deny that they were Jews. These writers knew the Old Testament well and made frequent use of it.

The New Testament, like all religious books, is full of repetition. For that reason the reading of religious books, from cover to cover, requires a good deal of patience. But this patience is often well rewarded. Quite unexpectedly we come across passages of extraordinary beauty. And not only beauty, but some of them so grip you with their straightforwardness, that not hundreds of years stand between you and them, but a day or two. As an example let me cite a passage from I Corinthians 16:21: "I, Paul, write this greeting with my own hand." Before us is reenacted the scene of the writer writing his letter. In order that it may be even more intimate, he adds a postscript in his own handwriting.

Throughout the Gospels there shines the personality of a young, philosophic and idealistic prophet, and in the rest of the books there pass before us unusual people and events. How towering is the personality of Paul in the Acts of the Apostles! How moving his self-accusation of the time he hounded and killed the first Jewish Christians without compunction or pity!

Christian sources contend that Jesus is the center of the world's history. Let us rephrase this somewhat: one of the centers—unquestionably. And so also is the New Testament one of the most important books in the world. How then can we Jews afford to ignore it?

Glorious Things of Thee are Spoken

J. NEWTON F. J. HAYDN

צִיון, שטאָט פון אונדזער גאָט דו

1 צִיון, שטאָט פון אונדזער גאָט, דו,
ס'ווערט פון דיר דערציילט דײַן פּראַכט.
ער, וואָס זאָגט און ס'ווערט, ער האָט דאָ
פאַר זײַן וואוינאָרט דיך געמאַכט;
פעסטגעשטעלט אויף פעלז פון דורות –
וואָס קאָן רירן דיך פון שטאַנד?
רונד פאַרשאַנצט מיט ווענט, דעם בּוֹרֵאס –
מעגסטו לאַכן פון די פײַנט.

2 שטראָמען פון דעם לעבנס־וואַסער
קוואַלן פון גאָטס ליבשאַפט אויס,
זעטיקן די זין און טעכטער,
ס'מאַנגלט נישט אין קיינעמס הויז.
ווען דאַרשט, אַז אַזאַ וואַסער
טרינקט אָן אַלצדינג אין דעם לויף?
חֶסֶד פון דעם האַר, דעם געבער,
אייביק פליסט און הערט נישט אויף.

3 פאַר אַ יעדער וואוינונג הויערן
וואָלקנזײַל און פײַערזײַל,
פאַר אַ הערלעכער באַשירמונג,
ווײַזן, גאָט אין מיטן ווײַלט.
צִיון, שטאָט פון אונדזער גאָט, דו,
ס'ווערט פון דיר דערציילט דײַן פּראַכט.
ער, וואָס זאָגט און ס'ווערט, ער האָט דאָ
פאַר זײַן וואוינאָרט דיך געמאַכט.

A Jewish Knight-Errant

Saul of Tarsus was a Jew who was not ashamed of his racial origin. Great men never are. Frederick Nietzsche, the stormy petrel of the 19th century, characterized him as "that eternal Jew *par excellence*," and Michael Cervantes, of Don Quixote fame, dubbed him a "Jewish knight-errant."

And yet though a Jew, the American Government reared him a monument in the rotunda of the Congressional Library at Washington; though a pupil of the illustrious Rabban Gamaliel, England built him the most costly shrine of her Empire—the Cathedral of St. Paul; though a Jew, or as he styles himself, "a Hebrew of the Hebrews," Felix Mendelssohn was inspired by him to write the musical masterpiece, the Oratorio of St. Paul.

Sholem Asch found in Saul of Tarsus a subject for a most intriguing novel, "The Apostle," which became a best seller.

Professor Joseph Klausner, long associated with the Hebrew University of Jerusalem, held that the dynamic personality of Paul was responsible for spreading the Messianic faith which centered in Jesus; and that no Jewish scholar dare ignore that flaming enthusiast whose ideas and expressions are so lofty that no nation and no tongue can do without them.

How much do we Jews know of this man who set the world agog? Isaac Meyer Wise, the founder of Reform Judaism in America, held that Saul of Tarsus was Elisha ben Avuyah, or Aḥer, because of the similarity of their make-up. Both were intellectually honest, both loved truth at the cost of popularity and even life itself.

The life story of Saul of Tarsus, of his early manhood spent at the rabbinical academy of Gamaliel; later as a bigot hounding to death every Jew who believed in Jesus as the Messiah; and then proclaiming the Gospel to every race and kindred of men—this life story, unrivalled for action and romance, the story of a great Jew, is delineated for us on the pages of the most noted book in the world—the New Testament!

The Roots of War

What causes wars and quarrels among you? Do they not spring from conflicting passions within yourselves? You want something which you cannot have, and so you kill; you are envious and cannot attain your ambition, and so you quarrel and fight. You do not get what you want because you do not pray for it. Or, if you do, your requests are not granted because you pray from wrong motives, to spend what you get on your own pleasures.

You false, unfaithful creatures! Do you not know that love of the world is enmity to God? Whoever chooses to be a friend of the world makes himself an enemy of God. Or do you suppose that Scripture has no meaning when it says, "He yearns jealously over the spirit which he made to dwell in us"? And yet the grace he gives is stronger. Thus Scripture says, "God opposes the proud and gives grace to the humble."

Submit yourselves then to God. Resist the devil and he will flee from you. Draw near to God and he will draw near to you. Sinners, cleanse your hands, and you who are double-minded, purify your hearts. Be sorrowful, mourn and weep. Let your laughter be turned to mourning and your joy to gloom. Humble yourselves before God and he will exalt you.

Brothers, do not speak evil against one another. He who speaks evil against a brother or judges his brother, speaks evil against the Torah and judges the Torah. But if you judge the Torah, you are not keeping it but sitting in judgment upon it. There is one lawgiver and judge, he who is able to save life and destroy it. So who are you to judge your neighbor?

Come now, you who say, "Today or tomorrow we will go to such and such a town and spend a year there trading and making money." Yet you have no idea what tomorrow will bring. Your life, what is it? You are no more than a mist, seen for a little while and then vanishing. What you ought to say is: "If it be the Lord's will, we shall live to do this or that." But instead, you boast and brag, and all such boasting is wrong. Well then, the man who knows the good he ought to do and does not do it is a sinner.—*The Epistle of James*, chapter 4

"I Am Not Alone"

John Cournos was born into an Orthodox Jewish home in Czarist Russia. As a child he had much to suffer from ignorant Gentiles who called him "Christ-killer." The impressions of childhood left an indelible mark on his mind. Since so-called Christians hated Jews, Cournos in turn hated Christ.

He was a mature man and had made a name for himself in literature, having some six novels to his credit, besides several plays, a volume of poetry, a biography, and many short stories, when he took up the reading of the New Testament. To his amazement he found that the Christianity of Russia had little in common with the teachings of Jesus. The Christians of Russia hated Jews, and Jesus was not only a Jew, but made love towards fellowman, regardless of race, a prime requisite.

We quote a few paragraphs from Cournos' book, An Open Letter to Jews and Christians:

"It took me fifty years to arrive at this idea, taking into consideration the fact that I began at its other end, and in direct opposition to it, and that my experience has not been primarily a bookish one. Things rooted in childhood have deep roots, to be measured by the years they have been nourished.

"It may seem an even greater wonder that now, after a lapse of nearly fifty years, I should feel the strongest compulsion to step boldly out into the open and affirm with a deep conviction which has been slowly and inevitably growing upon me—until silence is out of the question—that the time has come, is indeed ripe, for the Jews to reclaim Jesus and to reinterpret him.

"I am not alone, however, in arriving at the inevitable conclusion . . . I know a number of Jews who believe as I do, who believe that it is time that the Jews reclaimed Jesus, and that it is desirable that they should do so. Some of them hesitate to speak, lest their own people disclaim them.

"A great Jewish novelist said to me a year or two ago: 'The Jews should come to terms with Christianity.' These persons, it will be said, are intellectuals and do not represent Jewry. I reject this notion, because, to take three examples among them, one is a novelist whose books are about Jews and read by Jews; one is an educator whose work is among Jews and who knows Jews exceptionally well; and one is a scholar interested in Jewish Sunday Schools—if he were permitted by the elders he would include among his readings of 'gems' of Jewish literature the Sermon on the Mount.

"The rabbis should frankly and openly affirm that Christ is our own, our very own, flesh of our flesh, and bone of our bone, and he came not 'to destroy the Law or the prophets . . . but to fulfill.' He is our Prophet, our greatest prophet, the keystone of our ultimate faith."

The Song of Zechariah Ha-Cohen

Blessed be the Lord God of Israel!
For he has visited and redeemed his people,
And has raised up a horn of salvation for us
In the house of his servant David.
As he spoke by the mouth of his holy prophets from of old,
That we should be saved from our enemies,
And from the hand of all who hate us;
To show mercy to our fathers,
And to remember his holy covenant,
The oath which he swore to our father Abraham,
That we should be delivered from the hand of our enemies,
And should serve him in holiness and righteousness unafraid,
All the days of our life.
And you, my child, shall be called prophet of the Most High,
For you will go before the Lord to prepare his way,
To give knowledge of salvation to his people
In the forgiveness of their sins,
Through the tender mercy of our God,
Whereby the day shall dawn upon us from on high,
To give light to those who sit in darkness
And in the shadow of death,
To guide our feet into the way of peace.

The Gospel According to Luke 1:68-79

Samuel Isaac Joseph Schereschewsky

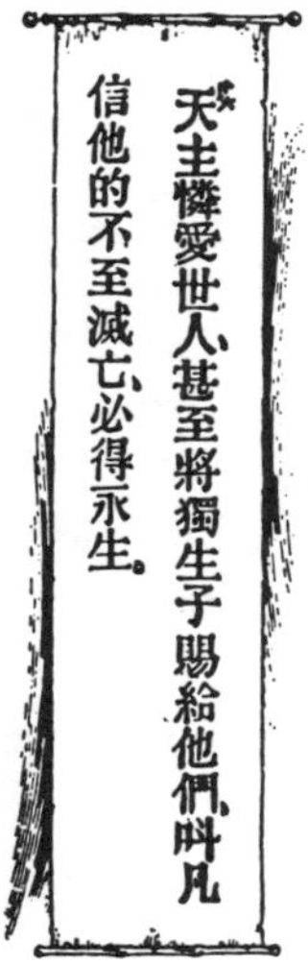

JOHN 3:16
IN MANDARIN

Founder of St. John's University, Shanghai, and Translator of the Bible into the Mandarin and Wenli Dialects

"Among the men and women who considered it their blessed work to bring the Word of God within the reach of far-off tribes by means of translations in their native idioms we may single out Bishop Schereschewsky, the 'Christian Jew.'"—*Rabbi Max L. Margolis,* EDITOR-IN-CHIEF OF THE HOLY SCRIPTURES FOR THE JEWISH PUBLICATION SOCIETY OF AMERICA.

"He was one of the six most learned Orientalists in the world."—*Max Muller,* PHILOLOGIST, OXFORD UNIVERSITY.

"The story of his life is one of the romances of the history of the Bible."—*Henry Otis Dwight,* THE CENTENNIAL HISTORY OF THE AMERICAN BIBLE SOCIETY.

Bishop Schereschewsky in His Study

In Life and in Death

Orthodox Judaism

Rabban Joḥanan ben Zakhai was lying on his death bed. His disciples came to visit him. When he saw them, tears filled his eyes and he cried bitterly.

"Rabbi," exclaimed the astonished disciples, "dost thou cry! Thou, the light of Israel, the right-hand pillar of the Temple, the mighty analyzer of the Law?"

"Ah, my children," sobbed the dying sage, "would I not weep if I were at this moment brought before an earthly king, who may be in his grave tomorrow; whose anger and the punishment he might inflict could not last forever, and who might be moved to pity by words of entreaty, or be pacified with a gift? You ask me why I weep, when I am about to be led into the presence of the King of Kings, Who lives forever, Who will not be moved to pity by words of entreaty or be pacified by the offer of a gift! There are two ways before me, one leading to Paradise, the other to Gehenna, and I know not whither I am going" (*Berakoth* 28*b*).

Reform Judaism

Emanuel Deutsch, a noted Reform Jew, wrote a book entitled WHAT IS THE TALMUD? In it he tried to show that Jesus was a plagiarist, that he copied from the rabbis. When Dr. Deutsch was at the height of his popularity his health gave way, and when he realized that he was fighting a losing battle, he wrote this confession in his diary:

"I cannot take comfort in the thought of death—I want to live—there is so much life, hot, full life within—that it shrinks from darkness and deadness. I envy those who can fly on the mind's wings to this harbor of refuge; I cannot follow, but keep tossing outside in my broken craft, through foam, and rock, and mist." LITERARY REMAINS OF EMANUEL DEUTSCH, p. 12

Messianic Judaism

We turn from the foregoing dismal pictures to the bright anticipation with which Saul of Tarsus, a pupil of the illustrious Rabban Gamaliel, looked forward to death. To him it was not something terrible, something to be dreaded. To him even a martyr's death was but the gateway to glory such as no mind can conceive. As the end of his earthly career approaches he writes:

"I am now ready to be offered, and the time of my departure is at hand. I have fought a good fight, I have finished my course, I have kept the faith; henceforth there is laid up for me a crown of righteousness, which the Lord, the righteous judge, shall give me at that day; and not to me only, but also to all them that love his appearing" (II *Timothy* 4:6-8).

"O death, where is thy sting?
O grave, where is thy victory?"
(I *Corinthians* 15:55)

A Lamed-Vovnik

Hayim Yedidiah Lucky was one of the most remarkable men I have ever known. I first heard of him in 1911 when I came upon his Hebrew journal, *Eduth l'Yisrael*. The make-up of the paper greatly intrigued me, and a letter to the editor resulted in correspondence between us. A year later I went to Stanislau, Austria, and met Lucky face to face.

Lucky was then about sixty years of age, and his gentle eyes, high forehead, and silvery white beard reminded me of a prophet of old. I soon realized that he was a learned man, equally at home in the Talmud and Bible, as well as in the whole range of Jewish literature.

During our meeting I remarked that on my way to Stanislau I talked to a Christian about the ideas propounded in *Eduth l'Yisrael*. "How do you know he was a Christian?" Lucky asked. "The fact that one is a Gentile does not mean that he is a Christian."

When I questioned how he, a Jew, could believe in Jesus, a smile came over his face. "I have been asked this many times," he began, "and it is because I am a Jew, who conscientiously tries to live according to the Law of Moses and the prophets, that I believe the Messianic hope of Israel has been fulfilled in Jesus. Many call me a convert, a proselyte. That is not true. I have not gone *over* to the Gentiles—Jesus is flesh of our flesh and bone of our bone."

"Are there many who hold your ideas?" I asked. Thoughtfully he replied, "There are quite a few."

This was an understatement, for Lucky was the focal point of an active movement made up of rabbis, writers, and others who sought to restore Jesus into the Jewish framework.

Lucky passed away at the beginning of World War I. His followers, though accepting the Messiahship of Jesus, never severed their connection with the Jewish community, and many perished in the Hitler holocaust.

Professor M. Weisberg, author of THE HISTORY OF NEO-HEBREW LITERATURE, refers to Lucky as "a most interesting personality, and an idealist whom both Jews and Christians respected and loved. His manner of life was like that of a *Lamed-vovnik*"—(one of the thirty-six righteous men to whose piety, according to Jewish tradition, the world owes its continued existence).

העדות.

(עדות לישראל)

עדות־התורה והתעודה, על כל סגלות ישראל ויהודה

ספר עתי

נכון לכלי חפץ, ערוך מזמן וקבוע, לשומרי תורת משה ועדות ישוע,

יו"ל

לפי חוברות, במספר מסֻמנות, ולא לפי חדשים ועתים מזֻמנות.

מאת

הישראלי איש־המשיח, ידידי', בן אהרן,' המצליח.

ספר רביעי	Ch. Th. Lucky. המעריך.	חוברת ראשונה

אנשים אחים, שמעו נא!

(דבר אל אחביי המאמינים בישוע).

אנשים אחים, זה היום תחלת מעשי לחדש מלאכת העדות
אחרי אשר היתה נחבאה אל הכלים זה ארבע שנים, ואמרתי
אל לבי, טרם אני נגש אל המלאכה אדברה נא אליכם, אחי
המאמינים מבית ישראל, דבר בראשונה. — הן אנשים אחים
אנחנו, כמוכם כמוני מצור יהודה חוצבנו, בני יעקב אנחנו, ילדי
ישורון כולנו. כמוכם כמוני תלמידי המשיח אנחנו, כי נפקחו
עינינו, אחרי אשר הקשקשים נפלו מהן ונמצא את אשר עליו
נבאו משה וכל הנביאים. אחים אנחנו, גם אם לא כל דרכי
כדרכיכם ולא כל דעותי כדעותיכם. גם אם משמאילים מאוד
אתם לפי דעתי, עוד משפט וצדקה לנו לקרא „אחי" איש אל
רעהו, כי כולנו בני אומה אחת, וכולנו חוסים בצל ישוע־אנחנו,
אשר בו כולנו אחד (אל הגלטיים ג': כ"ח) לכן שאוני נא אם
כמצות שאול, שליח אדונינו, אעשה והוכח אוכיח אתכם היום.
הנה שאול, השליח הגדול, צונו להוכיח כאח את כל המתרפה
במעשי הטוב (השני' אל התסלוניקים ג': ט"ו), להזהיר ולהוכיח
איש את עמיתו יום יום, למען לא נפול במוקשי מרמת החטא
(אל העברים ג': י"ג), להתבונן איש אל עמיתו לעורר איש את
אחיו לאהבה ולמעשים טובים, ולהוכיח זה את זה בראותנו כי
קרוב היום, אחרי אשר לנו דרך חדשה, דרך חיים, דרך אשר

For I Know That My Redeemer Liveth

Shall the mole, in his night underground, call the beasts from the day-glare to flee?
Shall the owl charge the birds: "I am wise. Come, dwell in the shadows with me?"
Shall a man bind his eyes and proclaim: "It is vain that men weary to see!"

Let him walk in the gloom, whoso will; peace be with him. But whence is his right
To declare that the world is in darkness, because he has turned from the light,
Or to seek to o'ershadow my day with the pall of his self-chosen night?

I have listened, like David's great son, to the voice of the beast and the bird;
To the voice of the trees and the grass; yea, a voice from the stones I have heard;
And the sun and the moon and the stars in their courses, re-echo the word.

And one word speak the bird and the beast, and the
hyssop that springs in the wall,
And the cedar that lifts its proud head upon Lebanon,
stately and tall,
And the rocks, and the sea and the stars; and "Know"
is the message of all.

For the answer hath ever been nigh unto him who would
question and learn—
How to bring the stars near to his gaze; in what orbits
the planets must turn;
Why the apple must fall from the bough; what the fuel
that sun-fires burn.

Whence came life? In the rocks is it writ, and no Finger
hath graven it there?
Whence came light? Did its motions arise without
impulse? Will science declare,
That the law ruling all hath upsprung from NoMind,
that abideth NoWhere?

"Yea, I know!" cried the true man of old; and who-
soe'er wills it, may know.
"My Redeemer—He liveth!" I seek for a sign of His
presence, and lo,
As He spake to the light, and it was, so He speaks to
my soul—and I know!

Solomon Solis-Cohen

צו מיר, איך וועל פֿאַרגעלטן, זאָגט גאָט.

אויב אָבער דײַן שׂונא איז הונגעריק, שפּײַז אים; אויב ער איז דאָרשטיק,

גיב אים צו טרינקען; וואָרים מיט דעם טאָן אַזוי, וועסטו אָנהויפֿן

פֿײַעריקע קוילן אויף זײַן קאָפּ.

לאָז דיך נישט גובר זײַן פֿון דעם שלעכטן, נײַערט זײַ גובר דאָס

שלעכטע מיט גוטן.

דער בריוו צו די רוימער, קאַפּיטל י״ב

כּלָלים פֿון לעבּן

לאָז זײַן ליבשאַפֿט אָן חניפֿה,

האָט פֿײַנט דאָס, וואָס איז שלעכט, און באַהעפֿט זיך אָן דעם, וואָס איז גוט.

האָט ליב איינער דעם אַנדערן מיט ברידערלעכער ליבשאַפֿט, אין כּבֿוד האַלט פֿאַר בּילכער איינער דעם אַנדערן.

אין פֿלײַסיקייט, נישט פֿויל, גלײַיק אין גײַסט, דינענדיק גאָט.

זײַט פֿריילעך אין האָפֿענונג, געדולדיק אין אַ צָרה, האַלט כּסדר אין מתפּלל זײַן.

זײַט מנדב פֿאַר די באַדערפֿענישן פֿון די הייליקע, און איבערגעגעבן צו הכנסת־אורחים.

בּענטשט די, וואָס רודף איך; בּענטשט, און שעלט נישט.

פֿרייט אײַך מיט די, וואָס פֿרייען זיך, וויינט מיט די, וואָס וויינען.

לעבט אין אַחדות איינער מיט דעם אַנדערן.

טראַכט ניט פֿון הויכע זאַכן, נײַערט לאָזט אײַך אַראָפּ צו דעם, וואָס איז שפֿל.

האַלט אײַך נישט פֿאַר חכמים אין אײַערע אייגענע אויגן.

פֿאַרגעלט קיינעם נישט שלעכטס פֿאַר שלעכטס, נײַערט גיט אַכטונג אויף דעם, וואָס איז בּכּבֿודיק אין די אויגן פֿון אַלע מענטשן.

אויב עס איז מעגלעך, און אויף וויפֿל איר זענט בּיכולת, לעבט בּשלום מיט אַלע מענטשן.

זײַט אײַך נישט נוקם, באַליבטע, נײַערט מאַכט פּלאַץ פֿאַר דעם גרימצאָרן פֿון גאָט; וואָרים סע שטייט געשריבן: נקמה געהערט

RULES TO LIVE BY

Let love be genuine,

Hate what is evil, hold fast to what is good.

Love one another with brotherly affection, in honor preferring one another.

Do not be lazy in your work, but aglow with the spirit, serve the Lord.

Rejoice in your hope, be patient in tribulation, be constant in prayer.

Contribute to the needs of God's people, and practice hospitality.

Bless those who persecute you; bless and do not curse.

Rejoice with those who rejoice, and weep with those who weep.

Live in harmony with one another.

Do not be haughty, but associate with the lowly.

Never be conceited.

Repay no one evil for evil, but take thought for what is noble in the sight of all.

If possible, so far as it depends on you, live at peace with all men.

Beloved, do not seek revenge, but leave it to the wrath of God; for it is written, "Vengeance is mine, I will repay, says the Lord."

Therefore, if your enemy is hungry, feed him; if he is thirsty, give him to drink, for by so doing you will heap burning coals on his head.

Do not be overcome by evil, but overcome evil with good.

The Epistle to the Romans, chapter 12

The Wailing Place

They took from us the wailing place
At which we sobbed our story,
And mourned with sad, averted face
The days of vanished glory.

Those hallowed stones still wet with tears
In what was once our city,
With none to share our haunting fears,
Or come to offer pity.

A wailing place! And yet near by
Was born the wide world's gladness!
O tell me, House of Israel, why
This deep, unending sadness?

—*Max I. Reich*

There's a Light Upon the Hills

H. BURTON — HATIKVAH

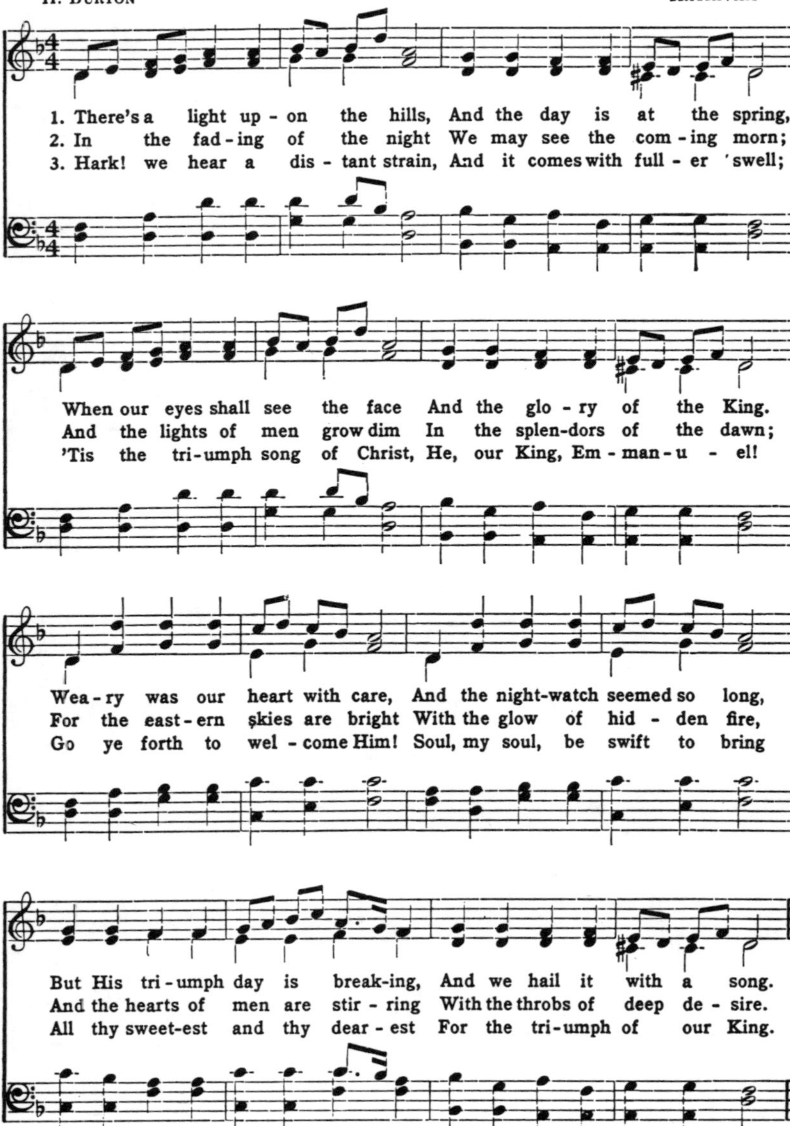

אויף די בערג שטייגט אויף אַ ליכט

1 אויף די בערג שטייגט אויף אַ ליכט,
און דער טאָג, ער ברעכט אַרײַן,
ווען מיר וועלן ס׳פּנים זען
פֿון דעם מֶלֶך און זײַן שײַן.
מיד איז אונדזער האַרץ פֿון זאָרג,
און די נאַכט־וואַך – לאַנג ווי לאַנג;
דאָך זײַן זיגער־טאָג קומט אָן איצט,
און מיר גריסן מיט געזאַנג.

2 אין פֿאַרבלײַכן פֿון דער נאַכט
זעען מיר דעם מאָרגנשײַן;
און די ליכט פֿון מענטשנס האַנט
גיי׳ן אין גלאַנץ פֿון מאָרגן אײַן.
ס׳גליט דער מִזרח־הימל שיין
מיט באַהאַלט׳נער פֿײַער־גלוט,
און דאָס האַרץ פֿון מענטשן וועקט זיך,
קלאַפּט מיט נײַעם, פֿרישן מוט.

3 האָרך! מיר הערן ווײַט אַ קלאַנג,
ער קומט נענטער, פֿול און העל;
ס׳איז דעם גואֵלס זיגער־ליד,
אונדזער האַר עִמָנוּאֵל!
גייט אַרויס באַגריסן אים!
זעל, מײַן זעל, זײַ פֿלינק און שנעל,
ברענג דאָס ליבסטע און דאָס בעסטע
פֿאַר דעם האַר עִמָנוּאֵל.

The Tenth Jew

By BEN AMI

Somewhere in France our division lay that night, the front three hundred yards away behind a small hill that hid us from the enemy's sight, but could not hide us from his guns.

Soaked and weary, we had driven ourselves fifteen miles in a forced march over muddy roads to the position we now held. Most of the men found what shelter they could in the wrecked homes and barns. Our two companies crawled into the remains of an old church.

Two of the church walls and part of the roof were still standing. The rest lay in crumbled ruins at our feet. Stones that had once reared themselves in Gothic grandeur mingled with the splintered remains of stained glass windows. Fortunately the wind was hurling the rain against the outer sides of the two walls. Curled up in the corner, we protected ourselves against the rain, but the cold slashed us like a sharp, steel knife.

Hour after hour we lay there, shivering, listening tautly for the intermittent whines of the great shells. The only human sound was Max's wracking cough. Max had been a shipping clerk in his uncle's dress factory. Drafted, he came to us wide-eyed and innocent. Seven months of shock-troop work had neither lessened his innocence nor hardened him. His cough was worse now than it had ever been. His slim body knarled and wracked itself with every spasm.

The shells came closer. With each explosion the church vibrated. The wind had shifted and the rain drenched us to our skins. We smoked cigarette after cigarette to keep warm. The rain doused the cigarettes before they were one-quarter smoked.

A messenger rushed in to tell us we were to move forward at five o'clock. At 4:20 Max died of an internal hemmorhage. Before he died he pleaded with us not to leave him unburied.

With sharp rocks we scooped out a shallow grave for him. Jacob, who had spent three years at a Rabbinical Seminary, was to perform the service. Suddenly we noticed that there were only nine of us, and Jacob insisted that we need ten, a *minyan.*

Silently we stood in the dim half-light of approaching dawn, the rain lashing our wet uniforms. Silently we stared at one another. The minutes ticked off. We needed ten Jews. In fifteen minutes we were to march. We needed ten Jews. The minutes ticked off. The dim light grew stronger. A shell burst nearby. The church vibrated to the explosion. A dull crash boomed behind us. Startled we turned to look. The statue of Jesus behind the shattered altar had toppled between two near-by pillars; the arms of the cross prevented the statue from falling.

Suddenly Jacob shouted, "Our *minyan* is complete!"

We stared at one another. Tears coursed down our cheeks to mingle with the rain as Jacob tenderly carried the statue of Jesus over to us and set it against the wall. Our *minyan* was complete. We had found the tenth Jew.

Slowly Jacob began the prayer: "*Yisgadal v'yiskadash sh'may rabo, b'olmo deevro hir'usay, v'yamleeh mal'husay* . . . ."

If . . .
I Would Be Proud

By HENRY A. PORTER

If I were a Jew I should feel that I have a right to be proud of the part played by my people in the drama of history.

"That Jew," men are sometimes guilty of saying with a note of scorn. They forget that behind "that Jew" there stand such names as have not been found among any other people.

Abraham and Moses are there—Abraham who defied idolatry when all the world was idolatrous, and Moses, the story of whose struggle for liberty steeled the hearts of the emancipators of the oppressed everywhere.

And David and Solomon are there—David the poet and Solomon the wise king. And Isaiah and Jeremiah and Ezekiel and Daniel are there—the prophets who dared to tell mighty potentates of their sins and foretell their doom.

Yes, and Jesus is there—Jesus before whom all Christendom bows in adoration. And Matthew is there, and John and Peter and Paul. These are but a few names pulled out of a glittering pile.

And as I think of these names and the history that lies behind them, I do not wonder that Disraeli, when Prime Minister of England, said in reply to some one who taunted him with being a Jew, "I can well afford to be a Jew. When your ancestors were naked savages in these islands, mine were princes in the Temple at Jerusalem."

If I were a Jew I would thrill at the New Testament description of the Jewish people as "Israelites, whose is the adoption, and the glory, and the covenants, and the giving of the Law, and the service of God, and of whom is Christ as concerning the flesh, who is over all, God blessed forever" (*Romans* 9:4, 5).

If I were a Jew I should wish my Gentile friends to recognize their debt to the Jews, their debt as Christians. What would our religion be without the Jews?

We owe the Jews our Bible. We owe them our Saviour, who in speaking to the Samaritan woman declared, "Salvation is of the Jews" (*John* 4:22).

If I were a Jew I would be proud of it.

The Touch

of the Master's Hand

'Twas battered and scarred, and the auctioneer
Thought it scarcely worth his while
To waste much time on the old violin,
But held it up with a smile—

"What am I bidden, good people," he cried,
"Who'll start the bidding for me?
A dollar, a dollar—then two, only two?
Two dollars and who'll make it three?

"Three dollars once, three dollars twice—
Going for three"—but no,
From the room far back, a bearded man
Came forward and picked up the bow.

Then wiping the dust from the old violin
And tightening up the strings,
He played a melody pure and sweet
As sweet as an angel sings.

The music ceased, and the auctioneer,
    With a voice that was quiet and low,
Said: "What am I bid for the old violin?"
    And he held it up with the bow.

"A thousand dollars and who'll make it two?
    Two thousand; who'll make it three?
Three thousand once, three thousand twice,
    And going and gone," said he.

The people cheered, but some of them cried,
    "We do not quite understand
What changed its worth." Soft came the reply:
    "The touch of a master's hand."

And many a man with a life out of tune,
    And battered and scarred with sin,
Is auctioned cheap to a thoughtless crowd,
    Much like the old violin.

A mess of pottage, a glass of wine,
    A game, and he travels on.
He is going once, and going twice,
    He is going and almost gone.

But the Master comes, and the foolish crowd
    Never can quite understand
The worth of a soul and the change that was wrought
    By the touch of the Master's hand.

Myra Brooks Welch

A Strange Synagogue Prayer

The folklore of a people is a mirror of its inner life. Sagas, traditions, runes, these are not merely the product of idle fancy; back of them lies history, the fortunes and misfortunes of tribal or group life.

It is but natural that Jewish history should have passed through stages similar to those of other peoples. The infiltration process to which practically every nation is subject has not left us unaffected. The names of our Hebrew months came from Babylon, and J. L. Peretz, an authority on matters Jewish, reminds us that "we have learned and adapted something from every nation, for we have lived among them all."

Doubtless it is little known how *Oz M'lifnai B'reshis*, one of the prayers for Yom Kippur, came to be incorporated into the Jewish Prayer Book. Students of our liturgy are of the opinion that the prayer is a Judeo-Christian infiltration into the poesy of the Synagogual liturgy, else what explanation is there for this strange petition from *Musaf l'Yom Kippur:*

"Our righteous Messiah has departed from us. We are horror-stricken and have none to justify us. Upon his shoulders he carried our sins, and through his wounds we find forgiveness. O, Eternal One, create him anew.

From Seir let come the Redeemer, from Mt. Lebanon let him proclaim redemption a second time through thy servant, Yinnon."

„פְּנָה מֶנּוּ מְשִׁיחַ צִדְקֵנוּ. פְּלַצְנוּ וְאֵין מִי לְצַדְּקֵנוּ. עֲוֹנוֹתֵינוּ וְעוֹל
פְּשָׁעֵנוּ. עוֹמֵס וְהוּא מְחוֹלָל מִפְּשָׁעֵינוּ. סוֹבֵל עַל שֶׁכֶם חַטֹּאתֵינוּ. סְלִיכָה
מְצָא לַעֲוֹנוֹתֵינוּ. נִרְפָּא לָנוּ בְּחַבּוּרָתוֹ. נָצַח בְּרִיָּה חֲדָשָׁה עֵת לִבְרֹאתוֹ.
מֵחוּג הַעֲלֵהוּ מִשֵּׂעִיר הַדְלֵהוּ. לְהַשְׁמִיעֵנוּ בְּהַר הַלְּבָנוֹן. שֵׁנִית בְּיַד יִנּוֹן."

Would the poet have voiced the above had he not felt that the prophecy of Isaiah 53, mirroring the great sufferer of the human race who brings redemption through his vicarious atonement, had been fulfilled in Jesus?

Why then is this fact kept from us? And why, it may be asked, is the prophecy of Isaiah 53 ignored in the *Haftorah* readings in connection with the Pentateuchal lessons? Yet there it stands, the choicest gem, the truest portrait of our Messiah in the whole prophetic volume!

ישעיה נ״ג

מִי הֶאֱמִין לִשְׁמֻעָתֵנוּ וּזְרוֹעַ יְהוָה עַל־מִי נִגְלָתָה׃ וַיַּעַל
כַּיּוֹנֵק לְפָנָיו וְכַשֹּׁרֶשׁ מֵאֶרֶץ צִיָּה לֹא־תֹאַר לוֹ וְלֹא הָדָר
וְנִרְאֵהוּ וְלֹא־מַרְאֶה וְנֶחְמְדֵהוּ׃ נִבְזֶה וַחֲדַל אִישִׁים אִישׁ
מַכְאֹבוֹת וִידוּעַ חֹלִי וּכְמַסְתֵּר פָּנִים מִמֶּנּוּ נִבְזֶה וְלֹא חֲשַׁבְנֻהוּ׃
אָכֵן חֳלָיֵנוּ הוּא נָשָׂא וּמַכְאֹבֵינוּ סְבָלָם וַאֲנַחְנוּ חֲשַׁבְנֻהוּ נָגוּעַ
מֻכֵּה אֱלֹהִים וּמְעֻנֶּה׃ וְהוּא מְחֹלָל מִפְּשָׁעֵנוּ מְדֻכָּא מֵעֲוֺנֹתֵינוּ
מוּסַר שְׁלוֹמֵנוּ עָלָיו וּבַחֲבֻרָתוֹ נִרְפָּא־לָנוּ׃ כֻּלָּנוּ כַּצֹּאן תָּעִינוּ
אִישׁ לְדַרְכּוֹ פָּנִינוּ וַיהוָה הִפְגִּיעַ בּוֹ אֵת עֲוֺן כֻּלָּנוּ׃ נִגַּשׂ וְהוּא
נַעֲנֶה וְלֹא יִפְתַּח־פִּיו כַּשֶּׂה לַטֶּבַח יוּבָל וּכְרָחֵל לִפְנֵי גֹזְזֶיהָ
נֶאֱלָמָה וְלֹא יִפְתַּח פִּיו׃ מֵעֹצֶר וּמִמִּשְׁפָּט לֻקָּח וְאֶת־דּוֹרוֹ
מִי יְשׂוֹחֵחַ כִּי נִגְזַר מֵאֶרֶץ חַיִּים מִפֶּשַׁע עַמִּי נֶגַע לָמוֹ׃ וַיִּתֵּן
אֶת־רְשָׁעִים קִבְרוֹ וְאֶת־עָשִׁיר בְּמֹתָיו עַל לֹא־חָמָס עָשָׂה
וְלֹא מִרְמָה בְּפִיו׃ וַיהוָה חָפֵץ דַּכְּאוֹ הֶחֱלִי אִם־תָּשִׂים אָשָׁם
נַפְשׁוֹ יִרְאֶה זֶרַע יַאֲרִיךְ יָמִים וְחֵפֶץ יְהוָה בְּיָדוֹ יִצְלָח׃ מֵעֲמַל
נַפְשׁוֹ יִרְאֶה יִשְׂבָּע בְּדַעְתּוֹ יַצְדִּיק צַדִּיק עַבְדִּי לָרַבִּים וַעֲוֺנֹתָם
הוּא יִסְבֹּל׃ לָכֵן אֲחַלֶּק־לוֹ בָרַבִּים וְאֶת־עֲצוּמִים יְחַלֵּק
שָׁלָל תַּחַת אֲשֶׁר הֶעֱרָה לַמָּוֶת נַפְשׁוֹ וְאֶת־פֹּשְׁעִים נִמְנָה וְהוּא
חֵטְא־רַבִּים נָשָׂא וְלַפֹּשְׁעִים יַפְגִּיעַ׃

A Star Among the Constellations

Millions of Jews have come and gone. There are some thirteen million Jews in the world today. Hundreds of Jews are born every twenty-four hours, and the ripple they make on the ocean of time is infinitesimal. Every so often a Jewish luminary lights up the sky—a Herzl, an Einstein, but like our system, they "have their day."

Midway in history there appeared a star among the constellations that has outshone all others—a Jew was born in the land of Israel. Other Jews were born in Israel, but the birth of *that* Jew has cut so deep a fissure in the centuries that it divided them into Before and After.

On the last day of each December our calendars become obsolete, and in their place a new cycle of days begins. Why? Because nineteen centuries ago, in the city of Bethlehem, Jesus entered upon the arena of history.

To the masses of our people Jesus is not the Messiah because he came contrary to their conceptions and expectations. The fantastic figure of a Messiah, who was to come on a striding white charger, beclouded our vision of the deeper meaning of Holy Writ. According to the Bible:

> The Messiah was to be born in the city of Bethlehem (*Micah* 5:1).
>
> He was to be a suffering Messiah (*Isaiah* 53).
>
> He was to go through humiliation and triumph over death (*Psalm* 16:10).

All this, and more. Why, then, do we not know it? Why do we not recognize Jesus as the Messiah? It is because our Bible is a sealed book to most of us.

Yet each recurring 25th day of December we face Christmas. Jewish shopkeepers and department store owners vie with Gentile buyers to make Christmas jollier and brighter, and all because on that day was born Jesus יֵשׁוּעַ–"a light to lighten the Gentiles, and the glory of his people Israel" (*Luke* 2:32).

Isaiah 53

Who has believed what we have heard? And to whom has the arm of the Lord been revealed?

For he grew up before him like a tender plant, and like a root out of dry ground; he had no form nor comeliness that we should look at him, and no beauty that we should desire him.

He was despised and rejected by men; a man of sorrows and acquainted with grief; and as for one from whom men hid their faces, he was despised and we esteemed him not.

Surely he has borne our griefs and carried our sorrows; yet we esteemed him stricken, smitten by God and afflicted.

But he was wounded for our transgressions, he was bruised for our iniquities; the chastisement of our peace was upon him, and with his stripes we are healed.

All we like sheep have gone astray; we have turned every one to his own way; and the Lord has laid on him the iniquity of us all.

He was oppressed and he was afflicted, yet he opened not his mouth; like a lamb that is led to the slaughter, and like a sheep that before its shearers is dumb, so he opened not his mouth.

By oppression and judgment he was taken away; and as for his generation, who considered that he was cut off out of the land of the living, stricken for the transgression of my people?

And they made his grave with the wicked, and with the rich his tomb; although he had done no violence, and there was no deceit in his mouth.

Yet it pleased the Lord to bruise him; he has put him to grief; when you shall make his soul an offering for sin, he shall see his seed, he shall prolong his days, and the pleasure of the Lord shall prosper in his hand.

He shall see of the travail of his soul and be satisfied; by his knowledge shall the righteous one, my servant, justify many, and he shall bear their iniquities.

Therefore will I divide him a portion with the great, and he shall divide the spoil with the strong; because he poured out his soul unto death, and was numbered with the transgressors; yet he bore the sin of many, and made intercession with the transgressors.

שחִיטה, און ווי אַ שאָף איז שטום פאַר איר שערער, האָט ער זײַן מויל נישט געעפנט.

דורך דריקונג און שטראָף איז ער אַוועקגענומען געוואָרן, און ווער פון זײַן דור טוט גאָר קלערן, אַז ער איז פאַרשניטן געוואָרן פון לאַנד פון די לעבעדיקע, פאַר די זינד פון מײַן פאָלק, וואָס האָט די שטראָף פאַרדינט.

און ער האָט געמאַכט זײַן קֶבר מיט רשָעים און רײַכע, הגם ער האָט קיין אומרעכט נישט געטאָן, און קיין פאַלשקײַט איז נישט געווען אין זײַן מויל.

אָבער גאָט האָט אים געוואָלט צעשטויסן דורך קראַנקשאַפט. ווען ער וועט מאַכן זײַן נֶפֶש אַ קָרבן, וועט ער זען זאָמען און פאַר־לענגערן זײַנע טעג, און דער רָצון פון גאָט וועט אין זײַן האַנט באַגליקן.

ליידן פון זײַן נֶפֶש וועט ער זיך אָנזען צו זאַט; מיט זײַן דער־קענונג וועט מײַן גערעכטער קנעכט גערעכט מאַכן אַ סך, און זייערע זינד וועט ער טראָגן.

דעריבער וועל איך אים געבן א חֵלֶק צווישן די גרויסע, און מיט די מעכטיקע וועט ער טיילן רויב; דערפאַר וואָס ער האָט אויסגעגאָסן זײַן נשמה צום טויט, און איז געציילט געוואָרן מיט פאַר־ברעכער, בעת ער האָט געטראָגן דעם חֵטא פון אַ סך, און זיך אָנגענומען פאַר די פאַרברעכער.

ישעיה נ״ג

ווער האָט געגלויבט וואָס מיר האָבן געהערט, און צו וועמען איז דער אָרעם פון גאָט אַנטפּלעקט געוואָרן?

וואָרים ער איז אויפגעגאַנגען ווי אַ יונג צווייַגל פאַר אים, און ווי אַ וואָרצל פון טרוקענער ערד; ער האָט נישט געהאַט קיין געשטאַלט און קיין שיינקייַט, אַז מיר זאָלן קוקן אויף אים, און קיין אויסזען, אַז ער זאָל אונדז געפעלן.

ער איז געווען פאַראַכט און אויסגעמיטן פון מענטשן, אַ מענטש פון פּייַן און געוואוינט צו קראַנקהייט, און ווי איינער פון וועמען מענטשן קערן אָפּ זייער פּנים; ער איז געווען פאַראַכט און מיר האָבן אים נישט געשוינט.

פאַרוואָר, ער האָט געליטן אונדזערע קראַנקהייטן, און אונדזערע ווייטאָקן האָט ער געטראָגן; מיר אָבער האָבן אים געהאַלטן פאַר אַ געפּלאָגטן פון גאָט, געשלאָגן און געפּייַניקט.

אָבער ער איז געווען פאַרוואונדעט צוליב אונדזער זינד, און צעשטויסן צוליב אונדזער אומגערעכטיקייט; די שטראָף פון אונדזער שלום איז געווען אויף אים, און דורך זייַנע בייַלן זענען מיר געהיילט געוואָרן.

מיר אַלע האָבן ווי שאָף פאַרבלאָנדזשעט, איטלעכער האָט זיך געקערט צו זייַן אייגענעם וועג; און גאָט האָט געלאָזט טרעפן אויף אים די זינד פון אונדז אַלעמען.

ער איז געוואָרן געפּייַניקט, און בעת ער האָט זיך געבויגן האָט ער זייַן מויל נישט געעפנט; ווי אַ לאַם וואָס ווערט געפירט צו דער

The Lord of Men Like Me

"The Lord our God, the Lord is one!"
The Word and Law replied
To me, who on Judea's hills
In spirit anguish cried.
As Hagar in the wilderness—
Oh, God—if God there be—
Unto my sick and wearied soul,
Reveal Thyself to me!

Is there no hope? Is there no peace
Where I despairing stray,
Among the stones and thistles
Of the desert's trackless way?
Thou who art throned in wond'rous might,
So distant, canst Thou see
The wretchedness, the bitterness
Of stricken men like me?

Upon the dark, forsaken night,
'Twas thus I cried, and, Lo
Came One, a Searcher, to my side,
Whose face was as the glow
Of summer's dawn, or as the peace
Of moonlight on the sea,
And said, "Oh, lost and pathless one
Come find the Way in Me."

I wonder, was He but a man
Of manger born and shame,
Or some bright Messenger who bore
The great Redeemer's name?
No crown adorned His gentle head,
But, oh! It seemed that He
Could understand the stricken thoughts
Of pathless men like me.

His fingers touched and healed my soul,
His presence stilled my fear;
No terrors hath the shadowed vale
For me when He is near.
They say He is a carpenter
That dwells by Galilee;
But whether He be God or man,
His spirit leadeth me.

Si Tannhauser

Come, Thou Long-Expected Jesus

C. Wesley — Eliyahu Hanavi

קום, דו לאַנג־געגאַרטער גואֵל

1 קום, דו לאַנג־געגאַרטער גואֵל,
לייז דיין פאָלק אויס פון דעם טאָל;
פון די שרעק און זינד באַפריי אונדז,
לאָז געפינען רו אַמאָל.

2 טרייסט און שטאַרקייט פון ישׂראל,
ביסט די האָפ'נונג פון דער וועלט,
ליבער וואונטש פון יעדער אומה,
פרייד פון יעטווידן געצעלט.

3 ביסט געבוירן צו דערלייזן,
ביסט אַ קינד, און דאָך—אַ ה
ביסט צו הערשן דאָ אויף שטענדי
ברענג דיין מלוכה—פריי פון צ

4 זאָל דיין הייל'קער גייסט באַהע
אונדז'רע הערצער אַלעמאָל;
אין דיין זכות זאָלסטו דערהייב
צו דיין טראָן אונדז פון דעם טאָ

The Talmud and the Gospels

No Jewish scholar can fail to recognize that the teaching of Jesus forms one of the most unique codes in the world. Dr. Joseph Klausner, for many years professor at the Hebrew University of Jerusalem, states in his epoch-making book, JESUS OF NAZARETH, HIS TIMES, HIS LIFE AND HIS TEACHING, that "in his ethical code there is a sublimity, distinctiveness and originality in form unparalleled in any other Hebrew ethical code."

Although Dr. Klausner admits distinctiveness and originality in the teaching of Jesus, he did not succeed in liberating himself from the general contention that this teaching has its basis in rabbinic literature. It cannot be denied that there exists a striking similarity between some of the teachings of Jesus and those of certain rabbis. But what basis is there for saying that it was Jesus and not the rabbis who indulged in plagiarism?

When the Talmud, in *Sanhedrin* 100*a*, attributes to Rabbi Meir the saying: "The measure which one measures will be measured out to him"—a saying identical in phraseology as well as in spirit with that uttered by Jesus in *Matthew* 7:2: "The measure you give will be the measure you get," Dr. Klausner elected to make of this a case for the rabbis. In the interest of historic accuracy it should be noted that Rabbi Meir was not yet born when Jesus gave wing to the above maxim.

Claude G. Montefiore, no mean an authority in matters Jewish, contended that "When Talmud and Gospels are compared, the originality is almost always on the side of the Gospels." This is no idle statement, but one which can be supported by evidence, as seen in the following parallels:

GOSPEL	TALMUD
Blessed are the merciful, for they shall obtain mercy. —*Matthew* 5:7	He who is merciful to others, shall receive mercy from Heaven.—R. Gamaliel Beribbi, 3rd century C.E. *Shabbath*, 151*b*
Let what you say be simply yes or no.—*Matthew* 5:37	Let your yes be yes, and your no be no.—R. Abaye, died 338 C.E. *Baba Metzia*, 49*a*
Why do you see the speck that is in your brother's eye, but do not notice the beam that is in your own eye?—*Matthew* 7:3	Do they say, take the splinter out of your eye, he will retort: "Remove the beam out of your own eye."—R. Johanan, surnamed Bar Napha, C.E. 199-279. *Baba Bathra*, 15*b*
Do not be anxious, saying, "What shall we eat?" or "What shall we drink?"—*Matthew* 6:31	Whoever has a piece of bread in his basket and says, "What shall I eat tomorrow?" belongs only to them who are little in faith.—R. Eliezer, died 117 C.E. *Sotah* 48*b*

The harvest is plentiful, but the laborers are few.—*Matthew* 9:37

The day is short, and the work is much; and the workmen are indolent, but the reward is much; and the Master of the House is insistent.—R. Tarfon, C.E. 120. *Aboth* 2:15

Freely you receive, freely give.—*Matthew* 10:8

Just as I teach gratuitously, so you should teach gratuitously.—R. Judah, 299 C.E. *Bekoroth* 29*a*

Whoever exalts himself will be humbled, and whoever humbles himself will be exalted.—*Matthew* 23:12

He who humbles himself for the Torah in this world is magnified in the next; and he who makes himself a servant to the Torah in this world becomes free in the next.—R. Jeremiah, died 250 C.E. *Baba Metzia*, 85*b*

Blessed are those who are persecuted for righteousness' sake, for theirs is the kingdom of heaven.—*Matthew* 5:10

Be rather of the persecuted than of the persecutors.—R. Abbahu, C.E. 279-310. *Baba Kamma*, 93*a*

The Sabbath was made for man, and not man for the Sabbath.—*Mark* 2:27

It (the Sabbath) is committed to your hands, not you to its hands.—R. Jonathan ben Joseph, flourished after the destruction of the Temple. *Yoma* 85*a*

How then may we account for the existence of parallels between the Gospels and the Talmud? Matthew, the writer of the first Gospel, relates that the fame of Jesus spread throughout the land, and that many people listened to him eagerly. There are also a number of references in the Talmud telling of discussions between Jewish Christians and leading rabbis, such as recorded in *Shabbath* 116*a*, *Aboda Zora* 16*b*, 17*a*, and 27*b*. Would not this indicate that the words of Jesus had become common property, passing from lip to lip, thus entering the Talmud and there sailing under false colors?

The Truth About the Rabbi

Max Wertheimer graduated from Hebrew Union College of Cincinnati, Ohio, in 1889, and became rabbi of B'nai Yeshurun Synagogue, Dayton, Ohio, where he served with marked success for ten years, esteemed and loved by all.

Possessing not only a degree of Bachelor of Hebrew Literature, Rabbi Wertheimer also had a Ph.D. from the University of Cincinnati. His name is listed as an alumnus of Hebrew Union College, and in fact his is the only Ph.D. in the CATALOGUE AND PROGRAM of 1897-1898, as well as in that of 1899-1900. From then on his name was dropped.

What happened?

In the NATIONAL JEWISH POST of November 25, 1955, Alfred A. Isaacs refers to Max Wertheimer as a graduate of Hebrew Union College who was disowned by his Alma Mater *for the sole reason that he became a Christian.*

It is generally assumed that a Jew becomes a Christian because he has been offered a job paying a fabulous sum of money. But let it be said—and this for the record—that as rabbi of B'nai Yeshurun Synagogue, Dr. Wertheimer received a salary of $2,000 a year, plus house, fees from weddings, bar mitzvahs, etc. When he became a believer in the Messiahship of Jesus he went back to school, after which he became pastor of

First Baptist Church of Ada, Ohio. What salary did he then get? The magnificent sum of $500 a year!

Thus it couldn't have been money which attracted Dr. Wertheimer. He was convinced, after much study and soul searching, that the Messianic predictions in the Hebrew Bible found their fulfillment in him of whom Moses and the prophets wrote, Jesus of Nazareth, the Messiah of Israel.

HEBREW UNION COLLEGE.

..CATALOGUE..

OF THE THREE DEPARTMENTS:

Preparatory • Rabbinical • Semitic,

... 1899 - 1900 ...

'93 Rabbi Abraham Simon, B. A., Omaha, Neb.
'94 Rabbi George J. Solomon, B. A., Vicksburg, Miss.
'93 Rabbi M. G. Solomon, B. L.
'84 Rabbi Joseph Stolz, D. D., Chicago, Ill.
'89 Rabbi Max Wertheimer, Ph. D.
'98 Rabbi Harry Weiss, B. A., Pueblo, Col.
'98 Rabbi Philip Wolf, B. A.
'99 Rabbi Louis Wolsey, B. A., Little Rock, Ark.
'99 Rabbi Martin Zielonka, B. A., Waco, Texas.

CINCINNATI,
COLLEGE BUILDING, 720 W. SIXTH STREET.

On the Mountain-Top Appearing

T. Kelly

Kohanim Negunim

אויף דעם באַרג באַווייזט זיך עמיץ

1 אויף דעם באַרג באַווײַזט זיך עמיץ,
דער מבֿשׂר קומט צו גיין,
גוטע נײַעס ברענגט ער צִיון,
וואָס איז לאַנג פאַרקנעכט געווען;
אָ געפאַנג׳נע!
דיך באַפרייט איצט גאָט אַליין.

2 נאַכט געווען איז לאַנג און טרויריק,
דײַנע פרײַנט – פאַלש, האַרט ווי שטיין;
איז געווען שטאָלץ דער שׂונא,
האָט געלאַכט בײַ דײַן געוויין?
הער אויף טרויערן, –
צִיון איז באַליבט און שיין.

3 גאָט, דײַן גאָט, וועט דיך אומקערן,
ער אַליין – וועט זײַן דײַן פרײַנט;
ס׳וועט פאַר דיר דער שׂונא שווינדן,
ס׳איז אַ סוף צום זיג פון פײַנט;
די דערלייזונג
שיקט דער האַר פון צִיון הײַנט.

UNDAUNTED HEROES

Money was not on their side. Government and public opinion were against them. Their Jewishness handicapped them at every turn. Yet despite all this they won out—those twelve Jews who started out from Jerusalem to bring countless millions under the wings of the God of Israel.

Let those who hold with Napoleon that "God is on the side of the heaviest battalions," remember that history knows of twelve men who pitted their lives against battalions, against wild beasts, the flame and the sword, to raise aloft the banner of a Jewish cause in a world that was hostile to everything Jewish. Undaunted

"They met the tyrant's brandished steel,
The lion's gory mane;
They bowed their necks the death to feel" . . .

The pagan could not understand these "God-intoxicated" Jews, and Jews who should have understood them, dismissed them as visionaries, chasing after a phantom. The centuries, however, have shown that no truer vision ever came to man than the Vision which led them on.

Strained as is the relation between Judaism and Christianity, the historic truth is that the warp and woof of Christianity were woven on the Jewish loom. Isadore Lhevinne indulged in no mere syllogism when he declared: "There remains this amazing, and so frequently overlooked truth: It is a lie that the Jews have rejected Christianity. Only a portion of Jews have rejected it. Had it not been for the other portion that went to death and exile there would have been no Christianity now."

The pages of the New Testament teem with incidents of Jewish activity among Jews and non-Jews in the interest of the Messianic movement of Jesus. What today is celebrated as Pentecost is but a harking back to that memorable *Shevuoth*, when 3,000 Jews allied themselves with the nascent movement and laid the foundation of a fellowship which has transcended race, time and clime. Inspired by the Messiah they carried the Torah and the message of the prophets beyond the confines of school and Temple.

The world is in sore need of another twelve Jews of like heroic mettle to raise aloft the banner of our glorious Messiah.

I Walk in the Holy City

I walk in the Holy City,
by pain and trembling tried,
as if a hidden wonder
walked by my side.—
And as I step on each stone
the voice of my heart I hear:
Gently! Here once did tread
a seer.

—Jacob David Kamzon

בְּעִיר הַקּוֹדֶשׁ אֲהַלֵּךְ

בְּעִיר הַקֹּדֶשׁ אֲהַלֵּךְ,
חִיל וָרֶטֶט צַעֲדִי,
כְּמוֹ פֶּלְאִי אֶחָד
יְהַלֵּךְ עַל יָדִי.—
וְעַל כָּל אֶבֶן כִּי אֶדְרֹךְ
אֶשְׁמַע קוֹל לְבָבִי:
לְאַט! פֹּה צָעַד
נָבִיא.

—יעקב דוד קמזון

When a Rabbi Met a Rabbi

In the third chapter of *The Gospel According to John* is recorded this conversation between Nicodemus and the Messiah.

Among the Pharisees there was a man named Nicodemus, a member of the Sanhedrin, who came to Jesus by night. "Rabbi," he said, "we know that you are a teacher who has come from God; for no one can do these signs of yours unless God were with him."

Jesus answered, "Believe me, no one can see the kingdom of God unless he is born again." Nicodemus said to him, "How can a man be born when he is old? Can he enter his mother's womb a second time and be born?"

"I assure you," said Jesus, "no one can enter the kingdom of God unless he is born from water and the Spirit. Flesh can give birth only to flesh; it is Spirit that gives birth to spirit. Do not wonder that I tell you, 'You must be born again.' The wind blows where it wills, and you hear its sound, but you do not know where it comes from or where it is going. It is the same with everyone who is born of the Spirit."

Nicodemus asked, "How can this be?" Jesus replied, "You do not understand this, you, a teacher of Israel? Believe me, we are speaking of what we know, and testify to what we have seen, and yet you refuse our witness. If you will not believe when I speak to you about things on earth, how will you believe if I speak to you about things in heaven? No one has gone up into heaven except the Son of man who came down from heaven. Indeed, as Moses lifted up the serpent in the wilderness (*Numbers* 21:9), just so the Son of man must be lifted up, that everyone who believes in him may have eternal life.

"For God so loved the world that he gave his only Son, that whoever believes in him should not perish, but have eternal life."

נישט אַרויפגעגאַנגען אין הימל אַרײַן, נײַערט דער, וואָס האָט אַראָפּגענידערט פון הימל, דער בֶּן־אָדָם, וואָס איז אין הימל. און אַזוי ווי מֹשה האָט אויפגעהויבן די שלאַנג אין דער מִדבר (במדבר כ״א, ט׳), פּונקט אַזוי מוז דער בֶּן־אָדָם אויפגעהויבן ווערן, כּדי יעדער איינער, וואָס גלויבט אין אים, זאָל האָבן אייביק לעבן.

וואָרים גאָט האָט אַזוי ליב געהאַט די וועלט, אַז ער האָט געגעבן זײַן בֶּן־יָחיד, כּדי יעדער איינער, וואָס גלויבט אין אים, זאָל נישט פֿאַרלוירן ווערן, נײַערט האָבן אייביק לעבן.

די בשׂורה לויט יוחנן, ג׳, א׳—ט״ז

אַ רֶבּי פֿרעגט אַ שאלה

און עס איז געווען אַ מענטש פֿון די פּרושים, וואָס האָט געהייסן נַקדימון, אַ שַׂר פֿון די ייִדן. דער דאָזיקער איז צו אים געקומען בײַנאַכט, און האָט צו אים געזאָגט: רֶבּי, מיר ווייסן, אַז דו ביסט אַ לערער, וואָס איז געקומען פֿון גאָט; וואָרים קיינער קאָן נישט טאָן די דאָזיקע וואונדער, וואָס דו טוסט, סײַדן גאָט איז מיט אים.

האָט יֵשוּעַ געענטפֿערט, און צו אים געזאָגט: פֿאַרוואָר, איך זאָג דיר, סײַדן איינער ווערט געבוירן אויפֿסנײַ, קאָן ער נישט זען דאָס מַלכות פֿון גאָט. זאָגט צו אים נַקדימון: וויאַזוי קאָן אַ מענטש געבוירן ווערן, ווען ער איז אַ זָקן? קאָן ער אַרײַנקומען אַ צווייט מאָל אין זײַן מוטערס טראַכט, און געבוירן ווערן?

האָט יֵשוּעַ געענטפֿערט: פֿאַרוואָר, איך זאָג דיר, סײַדן איינער ווערט געבוירן פֿון וואַסער און דעם גײַסט, קאָן ער נישט אַרײַנקומען אין דעם מַלכות פֿון גאָט. דאָס, וואָס איז געבוירן פֿון דעם פֿלייש, איז פֿלייש; און דאָס, וואָס איז געבוירן פֿון דעם גײַסט, איז גײַסט. חִידוש דיך נישט, וואָס איך האָב דיר געזאָגט: איר מוזט געבוירן ווערן אויפֿסנײַ. דער ווינט בלאָזט וואו ער וויל, און דו הערסט זײַן קול, אָבער דו ווייסט נישט פֿונוואַנען ער קומט, און וואוהין ער גייט. אַזוי איז יעדער איינער, וואָס איז געבוירן פֿון דעם גײַסט.

האָט נַקדימון צו אים געזאָגט: וויאַזוי קאָן דאָס זײַן? און יֵשוּעַ האָט געענטפֿערט, און צו אים געזאָגט: דו ביסט אַ לערער פֿון יִשׂרָאֵל, און דאָס פֿאַרשטייסטו נישט? פֿאַרוואָר, איך זאָג דיר: מיר רעדן דאָס, וואָס מיר ווייסן, און זאָגן עֵדות פֿונוועגן דעם, וואָס מיר האָבן געזען, און איר נעמט נישט אָן אונדזער עֵדות. אויב איך האָב צו אײַך גערעדט פֿונוועגן ערדישע זאַכן, און איר גלויבט נישט, וויאַזוי וועט איר גלויבן, אויב איך זאָל צו אײַך רעדן פֿונוועגן הימלישע זאַכן? און קיינער איז

$500,000 For a Jewish Book

When the Codex Sinaiticus, regarded as one of the world's most priceless manuscripts, was purchased by the British Museum from the Soviet Government for a half million dollars, Dr. A. S. W. Rosenbach, the famous Jewish bibliophile, is quoted as having said that a half million dollars for the fourth century parchment was "just giving it away."

The Codex Sinaiticus consists of the Septuagint, or Greek version of the Old Testament, the whole of the New Testament, the Epistle of Barnabas, and a part of the Shepherd of Hermas. The manuscript was discovered on Mount Sinai by the famous orientalist, Count Tischendorf. The Old Testament is not quite complete, but the New Testament is, thereby making it one of the most valuable ancient manuscripts extant.

As a Jew we plead guilty to a pardonable pride that this Jewish manuscript should be held in such veneration that nations vie for its possession.

Fortunately for most of us, we do not have to study ancient Greek, nor pay an exorbitant price to be in possession of the content of the Codex Sinaiticus. Its message has been translated into more than 1,000 languages and dialects, and can be purchased in any bookstore. One can get a Bible, for that is what the Codex

Sinaiticus is, in any language or style to suit one's pocket and taste.

But why bother with quaint manuscripts and still quainter books at this late date? To this Claude G. Montefiore, the Jewish scholar, would say: "If it is an improper ignorance not to have read some portions of Shakespeare or Milton, it is, I am inclined to think, a much more improper ignorance not to have read the Gospels." THE SYNOPTIC GOSPELS, Vol. I, p. 101

The Song of Love

If I speak with the tongues of men and of angels,
But have not love,
I am a noisy gong or a clanging cymbal.
And if I have the gift of prophecy,
And understand all mysteries and all knowledge,
And if I have all faith, so as to remove mountains,
But have not love,
I am nothing.
If I give away all I have,
And if I give my body to be burned,
But have not love,
I gain nothing.
Love is patient and kind,
Love is not jealous or boastful,
It is not arrogant or rude.
Love does not insist on its own way,
It is not irritable or resentful,
It does not rejoice at wrong,
But rejoices in the right.
Love bears all things, believes all things,
Hopes all things, endures all things.
Love never ends.
As for prophecies, they will pass away;
As for tongues, they will cease;
As for knowledge, it will pass away.

For our knowledge and our prophecy is imperfect;
But when the perfect comes,
The imperfect will pass away.
When I was a child, I spoke like a child,
I thought like a child, I reasoned like a child;
When I became a man I gave up childish ways.
For now we see in a mirror, dimly,
But then face to face.
Now I know in part,
Then I shall understand fully,
Even as I have been fully understood.
There are three things which last forever:
        Faith, hope and love,
But the greatest of them all is love.

I Corinthians, chapter 13

אֲבָל הַנְּבוּאוֹת תִּבָּטַלְנָה,
וְהַלְּשׁוֹנוֹת תִּכְלֶינָה,
וְהַדַּעַת תִּבָּטֵל.
כִּי־קְצָת הוּא שֶׁיָּדַעְנוּ,
וּקְצָת הוּא שֶׁנִּבֵּאנוּ,
וּכְבוֹא הַתָּמִים,
אָז עֲבוֹר תַּעֲבֹר הַקְּצָת.
בְּעוֹד יֶלֶד הָיִיתִי, דִּבַּרְתִּי כְּיֶלֶד,
בִּינוֹתִי כְּיֶלֶד, וְהָגִיתִי כְּיֶלֶד;
וְכַאֲשֶׁר הָיִיתִי לְאִישׁ, הֲסִרֹתִי מֵעָלַי דִּבְרֵי יַלְדוּת.
כִּי עַתָּה רֹאִים אֲנַחְנוּ בְּמַרְאָה, וּבְחִידוֹת,
וְאָז נִרְאֶה פָּנִים אֶל־פָּנִים.
עַתָּה יָדַעְתִּי חֵלֶק קָטֹן,
וְאָז אֵדַע, כַּאֲשֶׁר נוֹדַעְתִּי גַּם־אָנִי.
וְעַתָּה תַּעֲמֹדְנָה שָׁלֹשׁ־אֵלֶּה:
אֱמוּנָה, תִּקְוָה, וְאַהֲבָה,
וְהַגְּדוֹלָה שֶׁבָּהֶן – הָאַהֲבָה.

קוֹרִנְתִּיִּים א׳, י״ג

שיר של האהבה

אִם בִּלְשׁוֹנוֹת אֲנָשִׁים וּמַלְאָכִים אֲדַבֵּר,
וְאֵין בִּי אַהֲבָה,
הָיִיתִי כִּנְחשֶׁת הוֹמִיָּה אוֹ כְּצִלְצַל תְּרוּעָה.
וְאִם יֵשׁ בִּי נְבוּאָה,
וְכָל־רָז אֲנִי מֵבִין וְכָל־דַּעַת,
וְאִם יֵשׁ בִּי הָאֱמוּנָה כֻּלָּהּ, עַד לְהַעְתִּיק הָרִים מִמְּקוֹמָם,
וְאֵין בִּי אַהֲבָה,
אֲנִי אָז כְּאָיִן.
וְאִם־אֲחַלֵּק אֶת־כָּל־הוֹנִי,
וְאִם־אֶתֵּן אֶת גּוּפִי לִשְׂרֵפָה,
וְאֵין בִּי אַהֲבָה,
כָּל־זֹאת לֹא תוֹעִילֵנִי.
הָאַהֲבָה מַאֲרֶכֶת־אַף,
וְעֹשָׂה חֶסֶד הָאַהֲבָה,
לֹא תְקַנֵּא הָאַהֲבָה.
לֹא תִתְנַשֵּׂא וְלֹא תִלְבַּשׁ גֵּאוּת.
לֹא יִמָּצֵא בָהּ שֶׁמֶץ־דָּבָר.
וְלֹא תְבַקֵּשׁ אֵת אֲשֶׁר־לָהּ,
לֹא תִתְקַצֵּף וְלֹא תַחֲרֹשׁ רָעָה,
לֹא תִשְׂמַח בָּעַוְלָה,
כִּי עִם־הָאֱמֶת תִּשְׂמָח.
אֶת־כֹּל תִּשָּׂא, אֶת־כֹּל תַּאֲמִין,
אֶת־כֹּל תְּקַוֶּה, וְאֶת־כֹּל תִּסְבֹּל.
הָאַהֲבָה לֹא־תִבֹּל לְעוֹלָם.

Isaac Da Costa

Poet Laureate

Isaac Da Costa was a lineal descendant of the famous Jewish hero and martyr, Uriel Acosta. Next to Bilderdijk, he is considered the greatest poet of Holland.

This son of Israel was an ardent believer in the Messiahship of Jesus, and THE JEWISH ENCYCLOPEDIA says of him:

"Da Costa's character, no less than his genius, was respected by his contemporaries. To the end of his life he felt only reverence and love for his former coreligionists, was deeply interested in their past history, and often took their part."

The poem which follows was originally written in Dutch, and is generally assumed to have been translated into English by Henry Wadsworth Longfellow.

The Sabbath

On the seventh day reposing, lo! the great Creator stood–
Saw the glorious work accomplished–
Saw that is was good:–
Heaven, Earth, Man, and Beast have being:
Day and night their courses run.–
First Creation–infant Manhood–earliest Sabbath:–
It is done!

On the seventh day reposing, Jesus filled His sainted tomb,
From His spirit's toil retreating
While He broke man's fatal doom.
'Twas a new Creation bursting,
Brighter than the primal one.
'Twas Fulfilment–Reconcilement; 'tis Redemption:–
It is done!

On the Wings of Song

Felix Mendelssohn-Bartholdy was born in Hamburg, the grandson of the great Moses Mendelssohn, philosopher and Jewish reformer. Before he was 18 he produced his famous "Overture to the Midsummer Night's Dream," as well as the opera, "The Wedding of Camacho."

At the age of 28 Mendelssohn gave to the world the oratorio "St. Paul," and nine years later produced his masterpiece, the oratorio "Elijah."

Among his many compositions, "Songs Without Words" is perhaps the most admired, and who is not familiar with his "Wedding March" which invariably ushers in the bride.

Mendelssohn, brought up as a Christian, carried his Jewish heritage with great distinction. The poet Goethe was most impressed with "This wonderful grandson of *Nathan the Wise*, with gifts equal to Mozart's."

The Jewishness of Mendelssohn's music is dealt with at length in Marco Rothmuller's study on THE MUSIC OF THE JEWS. He quotes Max Brod, author and composer: "Outstanding among Mendelssohn's works is his violin concerto, which by its profound passion belongs among his most moving and beautiful creations. And it is just in this concerto that the Jewish note—albeit unconsciously used—can most clearly be heard, pervading the essence of the work rather than its details."

FROM THE ORATORIO ST. PAUL

Many of Mendelssohn's melodies were accepted by Central European Jewry, which considered them Jewish in content, and used them either as instrumental works or in arrangements adapted to the singing of various prayers in the synagogue.

Grove's DICTIONARY OF MUSIC AND MUSICIANS has this to say about the great composer: "It is generally noted that Mendelssohn possessed charm of manner to a high degree. For this and for his business acumen, his appreciation of domestic propriety, his punctuality, his sense of religious duty, and a somewhat moralizing attitude, he was indebted to his upbringing and to the ancient traditions of his Jewish race. He had a markedly Jewish appearance."

The life of Felix Mendelssohn, though of short duration—less than 39 years—was one of incessant activity. There is no question that both his talents and the character of his compositions were largely the product of his heredity and environment. After producing Bach's "Matthew" Passion Music with the help of his actor friend, Devrient, Felix said: "To think that it should be an actor and a Jew who give back to the people the greatest of Christian works."

Felix Mendelssohn-Bartholdy was indeed a noble son of Israel, a Jewish Christian whose life and work have greatly enriched the world.

The Return of the Exile

By JOTHAM GERIZIM

Even as nature abhors a vacuum, even as good abhors evil, so does Israel abhor exile. This feeling is expressed many times in our Holy Scriptures. There is passionate yearning for release from exile: "By the rivers of Babylon, there we sat down and wept, when we remembered Zion" . . . . There is joy in redemption from exile: "When the Lord turned again the captivity of Zion, we were like them that dream" . . . .

The same feeling is expressed on page after page of our Prayer Book. It is the very warp and woof of the tapestry of our people's life. On the Sabbath we say, "Thou didst deliver us from Egypt, O Lord our God, and didst release us from the house of bondage." And on the Sabbath before *Rosh Hodesh* we say, "May he speedily redeem us and gather our exiles from the four corners of the earth."

It is especially on Passover that our liturgy is rich in dreams of home. The four cups of wine are symbolical of deliverance from exile. "This year we observe the feast here. Next year may we be permitted to observe it in the land of Israel."

Physical exile is the reflection of spiritual exile—the spiritual exile of all humanity from its basic relationship to God and kindred.

Had not exile been experienced in the lives of our patriarchs? Abraham went into Egypt, and Isaac to Gerar. Jacob, too, had to flee to Paddan-Aram. Yet each of these exiles had a happy ending. The bondage in Egypt came to an end, and so did the Babylonian captivity. In this manner did God give us hope that the longest of Israel's exiles would also come to an end.

"I shall bring thy seed from the East, and gather thee from the West; I will say to the North: 'Give up,' and to the South: 'Keep not back,' bring my sons from far, and my daughters from the ends of the earth" (*Isaiah* 43:5, 6).

"Hear the word of the Lord, O nations, and declare it in the isles afar off, and say: 'He that scattered Israel will gather him' " (*Jeremiah* 31:10).

We see these promises being fulfilled in our day. From the east, from the west, from the north and from the south, our people are being gathered. Still, there is One of our people, the One Exile, the greatest of them all, who has not yet come home to his people. He is the Prince of Exile, the Prince of Peace. All Israel is to be gathered, and is Jesus not one of us?

As it is written in the Torah, Moses was not permitted to enter the promised land but died on Mount Nebo. Moses, the great leader of our people, died a lonely death and was buried in a lonely grave.

And so, being true to Moses, we should consider Jesus, for Jesus is as Jewish as Moses. Moses was born in Egypt, but Jesus was born in Bethlehem of Judea. Moses was brought up in an alien court, Jesus was brought up in a Jewish home. Moses was possibly an Egyptian name, but *Yeshua* is a thoroughly Jewish name, meaning "protection," "salvation," "one who saves."

"They that sow in tears shall reap in joy." These words taken from Psalm 126, which speak about the return from exile, have a special meaning. Jesus sowed in tears in Gat Shemen, in a garden overlooking Jerusalem. Now the desert is rejoicing again, and blossoming as the rose. So let us not be afraid. Let us let him in. Let us let him join us.

Many fiends in human form have desecrated his memory by calling themselves after him, and by pretending to act in his name. All their hatred cannot wash away his great love. Let him who shed tears amidst the olives reap in joy amidst the reclaimed desert's blossoming rose.

OTHER PUBLICATIONS

The New Testament in Yiddish

The Good News According to Matthew

The Man with the Book

Would I? Would You?

The Ox, The Ass, The Oyster

A Way in the Wilderness